MW01628436

# MY SUMMER CAMP JOURNAL

This Journal belongs to:

______________________________

I am ________ years old

This is me

Camp Name: ______________________

Camp Address: ______________________

______________________

Camp Telephone
Number: ______________________

This is my ______ year of camp

# CAMP MAP

Draw a map of the camp

# A MESSAGE FROM HOME

Your family can fill this out before you go on your adventure!

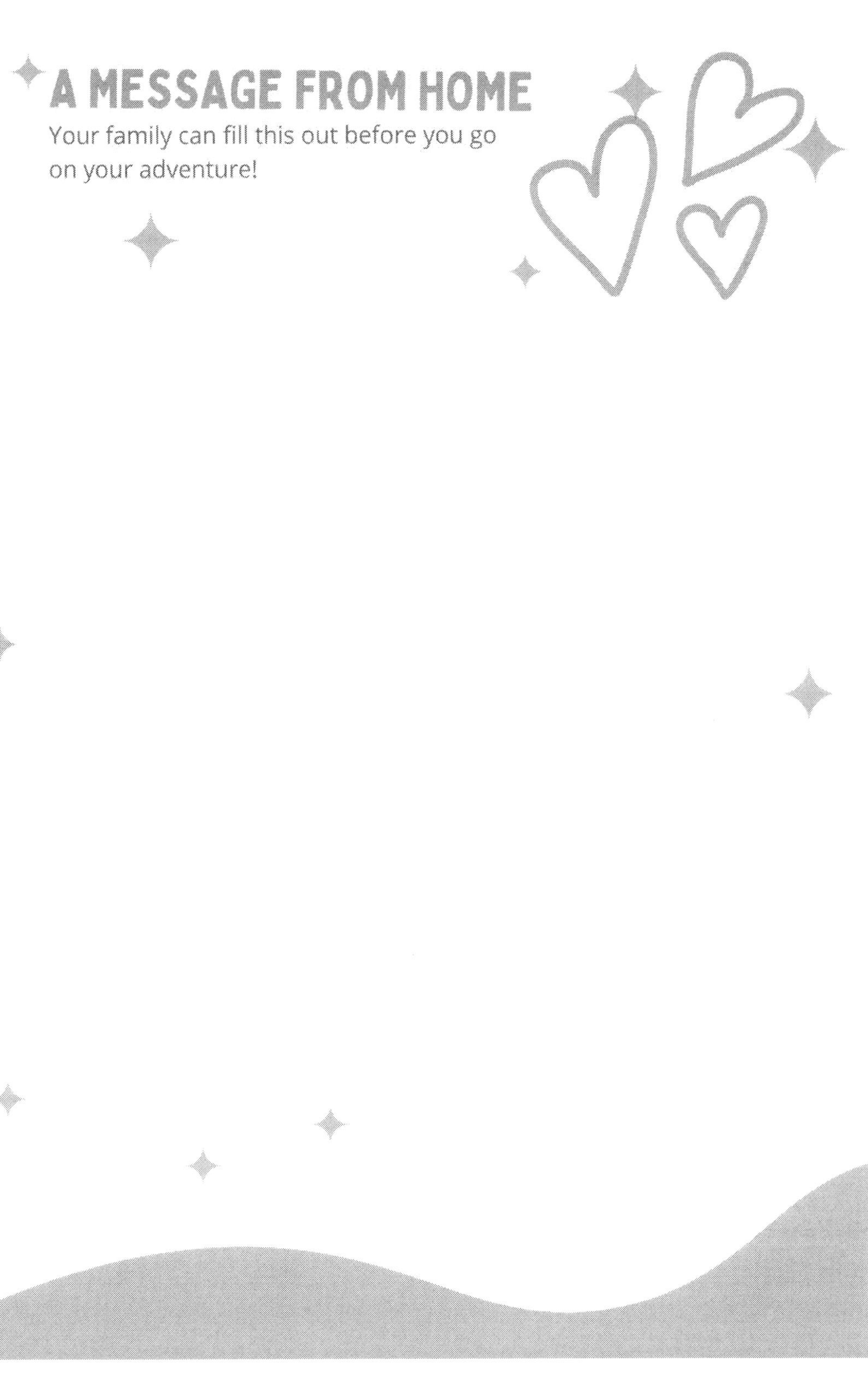

# ADDRESSES

To remember to write home

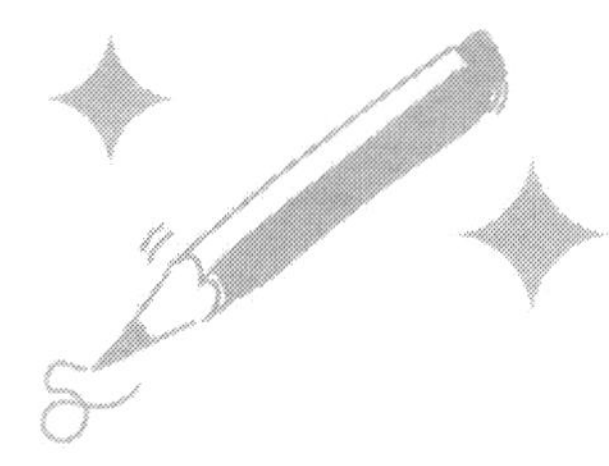

Name:

Address:

Number:

Email:

Name:

Address:

Number:

Email:

# ADDRESSES

To remember to write home

Name:

Address:

Number:

Email:

Name:

Address:

Number:

Email:

# ADDRESSES

To remember to write home

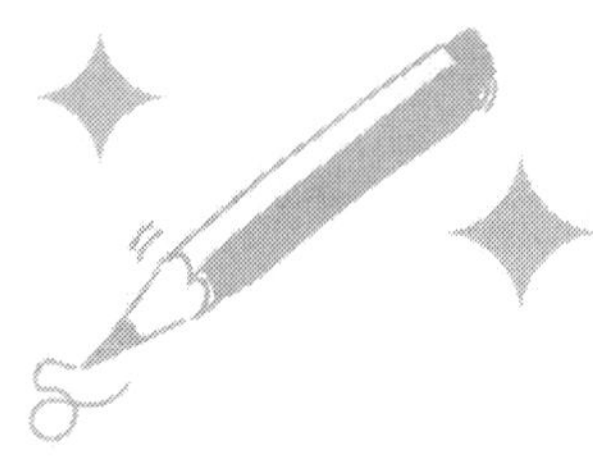

Name: ________________

Address: ________________

________________

Number: ________________

Email: ________________

Name: ________________

Address: ________________

________________

Number: ________________

Email: ________________

# ADDRESSES

To remember to write home

Name:

Address:

Number:

Email:

Name:

Address:

Number:

Email:

# ADDRESSES

To remember to write home

Name:

Address:

Number:

Email:

Name:

Address:

Number:

Email:

# PACKING LIST

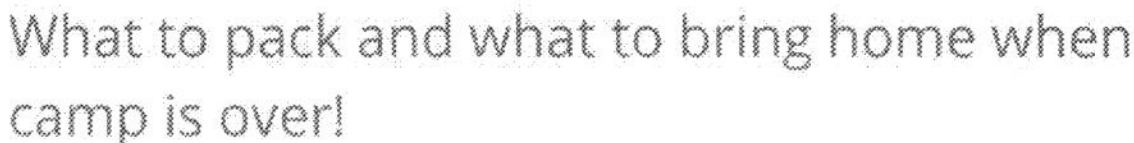

What to pack and what to bring home when camp is over!

## Bring to Camp

# PACKING LIST

What to pack and what to bring home when camp is over!

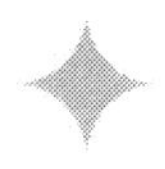

## Bring to Camp

# PACKING LIST

What to pack and what to bring home when camp is over!

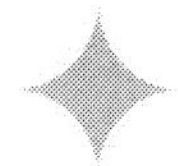
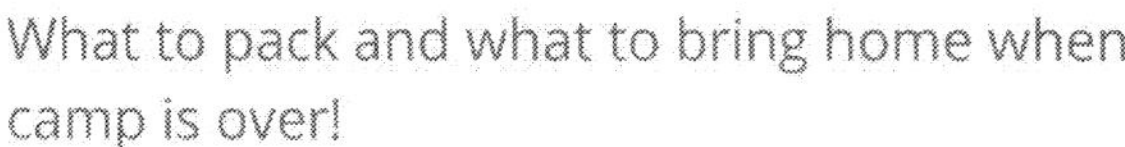

## Bring Home

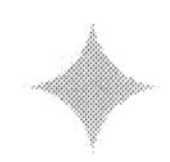

# PACKING LIST

What to pack and what to bring home when camp is over!

## Bring Home

# MY CAMPING PALS

To keep in touch with new friends

Name: ______________________________

Birthday: ______________________________

Address: ______________________________

______________________________

Number: ______________________________

Email & Social Media: ______________________________

______________________________

Name: ______________________________

Birthday: ______________________________

Address: ______________________________

______________________________

Number: ______________________________

Email & Social Media: ______________________________

______________________________

# MY CAMPING PALS

To keep in touch with new friends

Name: ________________________________

Birthday: ________________________________

Address: ________________________________

________________________________

Number: ________________________________

Email & Social Media: ________________________________

________________________________

Name: ________________________________

Birthday: ________________________________

Address: ________________________________

________________________________

Number: ________________________________

Email & Social Media: ________________________________

________________________________

# MY CAMPING PALS

To keep in touch with new friends

Name:

Birthday:

Address:

Number:

Email & Social Media:

Name:

Birthday:

Address:

Number:

Email & Social Media:

# MY CAMPING PALS

To keep in touch with new friends

Name: ______________________________

Birthday: ______________________________

Address: ______________________________

______________________________

Number: ______________________________

Email & Social Media: ______________________________

______________________________

Name: ______________________________

Birthday: ______________________________

Address: ______________________________

______________________________

Number: ______________________________

Email & Social Media: ______________________________

______________________________

# MY CAMPING PALS

To keep in touch with new friends

Name:

Birthday:

Address:

Number:

Email & Social Media:

Name:

Birthday:

Address:

Number:

Email & Social Media:

# MY CAMPING PALS

To keep in touch with new friends

Name:

Birthday:

Address:

Number:

Email & Social Media:

Name:

Birthday:

Address:

Number:

Email & Social Media:

# MY CAMPING PALS

To keep in touch with new friends

Name:

Birthday:

Address:

Number:

Email & Social Media:

Name:

Birthday:

Address:

Number:

Email & Social Media:

# MY CAMPING PALS

To keep in touch with new friends

Name:

Birthday:

Address:

Number:

Email & Social Media:

Name:

Birthday:

Address:

Number:

Email & Social Media:

# MY CAMPING PALS

To keep in touch with new friends

Name:

Birthday:

Address:

Number:

Email & Social Media:

Name:

Birthday:

Address:

Number:

Email & Social Media:

# MY CAMPING PALS

To keep in touch with new friends

Name:

Birthday:

Address:

Number:

Email & Social Media:

Name:

Birthday:

Address:

Number:

Email & Social Media:

# MY CAMPING PALS

To keep in touch with new friends

Name: ____________________

Birthday: ____________________

Address: ____________________

____________________

Number: ____________________

Email & Social Media: ____________________

____________________

Name: ____________________

Birthday: ____________________

Address: ____________________

____________________

Number: ____________________

Email & Social Media: ____________________

____________________

# CAMP QUOTES, SONGS & STUFF I WANT TO REMEMBER

# CAMP QUOTES, SONGS & STUFF I WANT TO REMEMBER

# CAMP QUOTES, SONGS & STUFF I WANT TO REMEMBER

# CAMP QUOTES, SONGS & STUFF I WANT TO REMEMBER

# CAMP QUOTES, SONGS & STUFF I WANT TO REMEMBER

# CAMP QUOTES, SONGS & STUFF I WANT TO REMEMBER

# CAMP QUOTES, SONGS & STUFF I WANT TO REMEMBER

# CAMP QUOTES, SONGS & STUFF I WANT TO REMEMBER

# JOURNAL NOTES

Highlights of the day, favorite meals,
funny moments, things I'd change if I had a do-over
and random thoughts

# JOURNAL NOTES

Highlights of the day, favorite meals,
funny moments, things I'd change if I had a do-over
and random thoughts

# JOURNAL NOTES

Highlights of the day, favorite meals,
funny moments, things I'd change if I had a do-over
and random thoughts

# JOURNAL NOTES

Highlights of the day, favorite meals,
funny moments, things I'd change if I had a do-over
and random thoughts

# JOURNAL NOTES

Highlights of the day, favorite meals,
funny moments, things I'd change if I had a do-over
and random thoughts

# JOURNAL NOTES

Highlights of the day, favorite meals,
funny moments, things I'd change if I had a do-over
and random thoughts

# JOURNAL NOTES

Highlights of the day, favorite meals,
funny moments, things I'd change if I had a do-over
and random thoughts

# JOURNAL NOTES

Highlights of the day, favorite meals,
funny moments, things I'd change if I had a do-over
and random thoughts

# JOURNAL NOTES

Highlights of the day, favorite meals,
funny moments, things I'd change if I had a do-over
and random thoughts

# JOURNAL NOTES

Highlights of the day, favorite meals,
funny moments, things I'd change if I had a do-over
and random thoughts

# JOURNAL NOTES

Highlights of the day, favorite meals,
funny moments, things I'd change if I had a do-over
and random thoughts

# JOURNAL NOTES

Highlights of the day, favorite meals,
funny moments, things I'd change if I had a do-over
and random thoughts

# JOURNAL NOTES

Highlights of the day, favorite meals,
funny moments, things I'd change if I had a do-over
and random thoughts

# JOURNAL NOTES

Highlights of the day, favorite meals,
funny moments, things I'd change if I had a do-over
and random thoughts

# JOURNAL NOTES

Highlights of the day, favorite meals,
funny moments, things I'd change if I had a do-over
and random thoughts

# JOURNAL NOTES

Highlights of the day, favorite meals,
funny moments, things I'd change if I had a do-over
and random thoughts

# JOURNAL NOTES

Highlights of the day, favorite meals,
funny moments, things I'd change if I had a do-over
and random thoughts

# JOURNAL NOTES

Highlights of the day, favorite meals,
funny moments, things I'd change if I had a do-over
and random thoughts

# JOURNAL NOTES

Highlights of the day, favorite meals,
funny moments, things I'd change if I had a do-over
and random thoughts

# JOURNAL NOTES

Highlights of the day, favorite meals, funny moments, things I'd change if I had a do-over and random thoughts

# JOURNAL NOTES

Highlights of the day, favorite meals,
funny moments, things I'd change if I had a do-over
and random thoughts

# JOURNAL NOTES

Highlights of the day, favorite meals,
funny moments, things I'd change if I had a do-over
and random thoughts

# JOURNAL NOTES

Highlights of the day, favorite meals,
funny moments, things I'd change if I had a do-over
and random thoughts

# JOURNAL NOTES

Highlights of the day, favorite meals,
funny moments, things I'd change if I had a do-over
and random thoughts

# JOURNAL NOTES

Highlights of the day, favorite meals,
funny moments, things I'd change if I had a do-over
and random thoughts

# JOURNAL NOTES

Highlights of the day, favorite meals,
funny moments, things I'd change if I had a do-over
and random thoughts

# JOURNAL NOTES

Highlights of the day, favorite meals,
funny moments, things I'd change if I had a do-over
and random thoughts

# JOURNAL NOTES

Highlights of the day, favorite meals,
funny moments, things I'd change if I had a do-over
and random thoughts

# JOURNAL NOTES

Highlights of the day, favorite meals,
funny moments, things I'd change if I had a do-over
and random thoughts

# JOURNAL NOTES

Highlights of the day, favorite meals,
funny moments, things I'd change if I had a do-over
and random thoughts

# JOURNAL NOTES

Highlights of the day, favorite meals,
funny moments, things I'd change if I had a do-over
and random thoughts

# JOURNAL NOTES

Highlights of the day, favorite meals,
funny moments, things I'd change if I had a do-over
and random thoughts

# JOURNAL NOTES

Highlights of the day, favorite meals,
funny moments, things I'd change if I had a do-over
and random thoughts

# JOURNAL NOTES

Highlights of the day, favorite meals,
funny moments, things I'd change if I had a do-over
and random thoughts

## JOURNAL NOTES

Highlights of the day, favorite meals,
funny moments, things I'd change if I had a do-over
and random thoughts

# JOURNAL NOTES

Highlights of the day, favorite meals,
funny moments, things I'd change if I had a do-over
and random thoughts

# JOURNAL NOTES

Highlights of the day, favorite meals,
funny moments, things I'd change if I had a do-over
and random thoughts

# JOURNAL NOTES

Highlights of the day, favorite meals,
funny moments, things I'd change if I had a do-over
and random thoughts

# JOURNAL NOTES

Highlights of the day, favorite meals,
funny moments, things I'd change if I had a do-over
and random thoughts

# JOURNAL NOTES

Highlights of the day, favorite meals,
funny moments, things I'd change if I had a do-over
and random thoughts

# JOURNAL NOTES

Highlights of the day, favorite meals,
funny moments, things I'd change if I had a do-over
and random thoughts

# JOURNAL NOTES

Highlights of the day, favorite meals,
funny moments, things I'd change if I had a do-over
and random thoughts

# JOURNAL NOTES

Highlights of the day, favorite meals,
funny moments, things I'd change if I had a do-over
and random thoughts

# JOURNAL NOTES

Highlights of the day, favorite meals, funny moments, things I'd change if I had a do-over and random thoughts

# JOURNAL NOTES

Highlights of the day, favorite meals,
funny moments, things I'd change if I had a do-over
and random thoughts

# JOURNAL NOTES

Highlights of the day, favorite meals,
funny moments, things I'd change if I had a do-over
and random thoughts

# JOURNAL NOTES

Highlights of the day, favorite meals,
funny moments, things I'd change if I had a do-over
and random thoughts

# JOURNAL NOTES

Highlights of the day, favorite meals,
funny moments, things I'd change if I had a do-over
and random thoughts

# JOURNAL NOTES

Highlights of the day, favorite meals,
funny moments, things I'd change if I had a do-over
and random thoughts

# JOURNAL NOTES

Highlights of the day, favorite meals,
funny moments, things I'd change if I had a do-over
and random thoughts

# JOURNAL NOTES

Highlights of the day, favorite meals,
funny moments, things I'd change if I had a do-over
and random thoughts

# JOURNAL NOTES

Highlights of the day, favorite meals,
funny moments, things I'd change if I had a do-over
and random thoughts

# JOURNAL NOTES

Highlights of the day, favorite meals,
funny moments, things I'd change if I had a do-over
and random thoughts

# JOURNAL NOTES

Highlights of the day, favorite meals,
funny moments, things I'd change if I had a do-over
and random thoughts

# JOURNAL NOTES

Highlights of the day, favorite meals,
funny moments, things I'd change if I had a do-over
and random thoughts

# JOURNAL NOTES

Highlights of the day, favorite meals,
funny moments, things I'd change if I had a do-over
and random thoughts

# JOURNAL NOTES

Highlights of the day, favorite meals,
funny moments, things I'd change if I had a do-over
and random thoughts

# JOURNAL NOTES

Highlights of the day, favorite meals, funny moments, things I'd change if I had a do-over and random thoughts

# JOURNAL NOTES

Highlights of the day, favorite meals,
funny moments, things I'd change if I had a do-over
and random thoughts

# JOURNAL NOTES

Highlights of the day, favorite meals,
funny moments, things I'd change if I had a do-over
and random thoughts

# JOURNAL NOTES

Highlights of the day, favorite meals,
funny moments, things I'd change if I had a do-over
and random thoughts

# JOURNAL NOTES

Highlights of the day, favorite meals,
funny moments, things I'd change if I had a do-over
and random thoughts

# JOURNAL NOTES

Highlights of the day, favorite meals,
funny moments, things I'd change if I had a do-over
and random thoughts

# JOURNAL NOTES

Highlights of the day, favorite meals,
funny moments, things I'd change if I had a do-over
and random thoughts

# JOURNAL NOTES

Highlights of the day, favorite meals,
funny moments, things I'd change if I had a do-over
and random thoughts

# JOURNAL NOTES

Highlights of the day, favorite meals,
funny moments, things I'd change if I had a do-over
and random thoughts

# JOURNAL NOTES

Highlights of the day, favorite meals,
funny moments, things I'd change if I had a do-over
and random thoughts

# JOURNAL NOTES

Highlights of the day, favorite meals,
funny moments, things I'd change if I had a do-over
and random thoughts

# JOURNAL NOTES

Highlights of the day, favorite meals,
funny moments, things I'd change if I had a do-over
and random thoughts

# JOURNAL NOTES

Highlights of the day, favorite meals,
funny moments, things I'd change if I had a do-over
and random thoughts

# JOURNAL NOTES

Highlights of the day, favorite meals,
funny moments, things I'd change if I had a do-over
and random thoughts

# JOURNAL NOTES

Highlights of the day, favorite meals,
funny moments, things I'd change if I had a do-over
and random thoughts

# JOURNAL NOTES

Highlights of the day, favorite meals,
funny moments, things I'd change if I had a do-over
and random thoughts

# JOURNAL NOTES

Highlights of the day, favorite meals,
funny moments, things I'd change if I had a do-over
and random thoughts

# JOURNAL NOTES

Highlights of the day, favorite meals,
funny moments, things I'd change if I had a do-over
and random thoughts

# JOURNAL NOTES

Highlights of the day, favorite meals,
funny moments, things I'd change if I had a do-over
and random thoughts

# JOURNAL NOTES

Highlights of the day, favorite meals,
funny moments, things I'd change if I had a do-over
and random thoughts

# JOURNAL NOTES

Highlights of the day, favorite meals,
funny moments, things I'd change if I had a do-over
and random thoughts

Made in United States
Orlando, FL
01 July 2022